Clothes

Boots and shoes

Pat Mackenzie

Oxford University Press

Wilf and Wilma need new shoes.

People wear all kinds of shoes.

This book tells you why.

Contents

Why you need shoes

Boots and shoes protect your feet.

They can keep your feet dry and warm.

You need to choose the right shoes.
Some shoes are for sport and
some are for play.

Indoors and outdoors

Indoor shoes are called slippers.
Slippers need to be soft and light.
They are often made out of cloth.

Leather boots are strong and waterproof.

Outdoor shoes need to be strong.
Leather and plastic are strong materials.
They are also waterproof.

Boots and shoes for sport

There are special shoes for sports.
Some have studs on the soles.
The studs can grip wet grass and mud.

studs

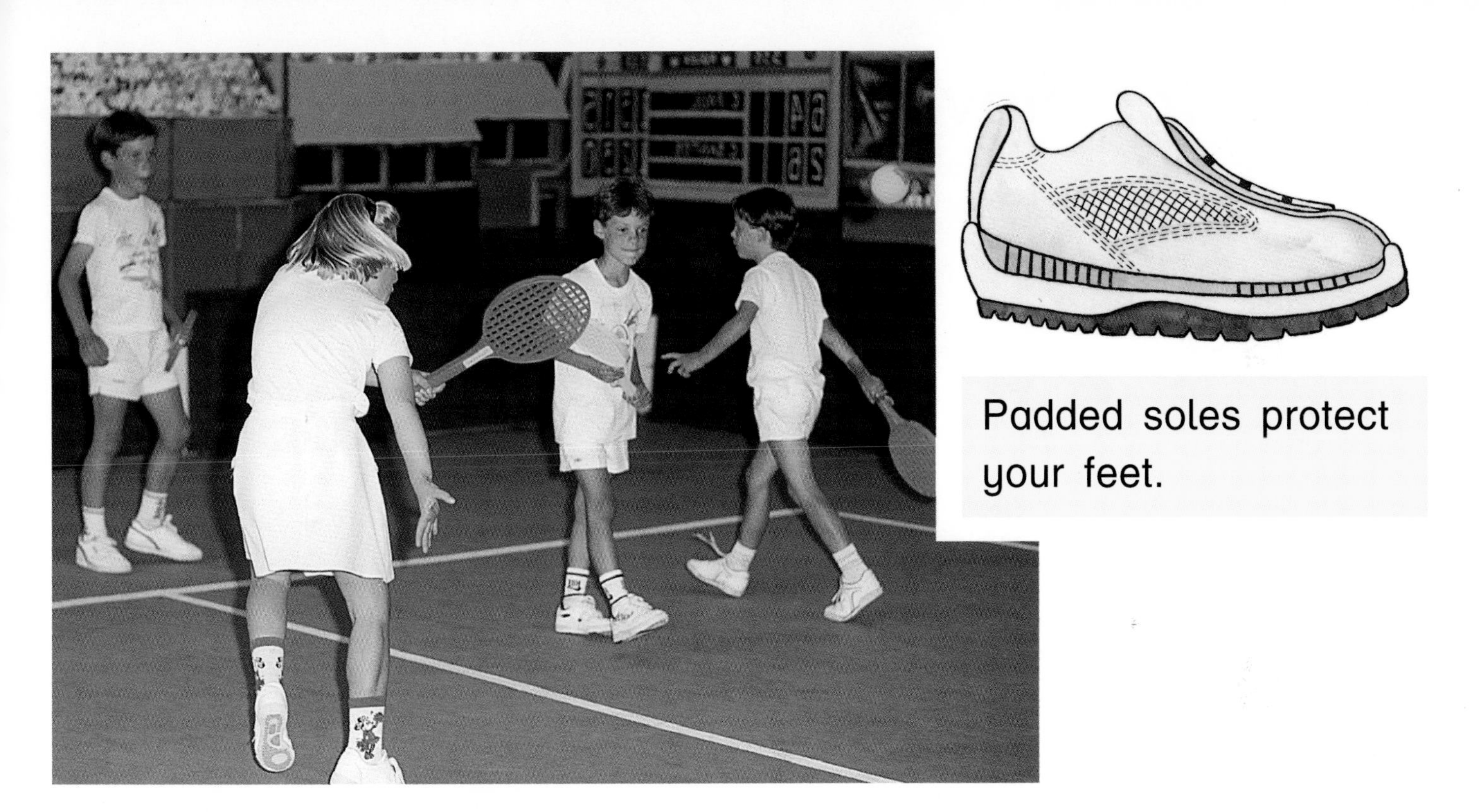

Padded soles protect your feet.

Trainers have padded soles.
The ridges on the soles grip the ground.
They stop you slipping.

Boots for moving around

You can move quickly in these boots.
Roller boots have wheels on the soles.
They work best on smooth ground.

Ice skates have blades on the soles.
The blades are made of metal.
You can glide over the ice.

Shoes around the world

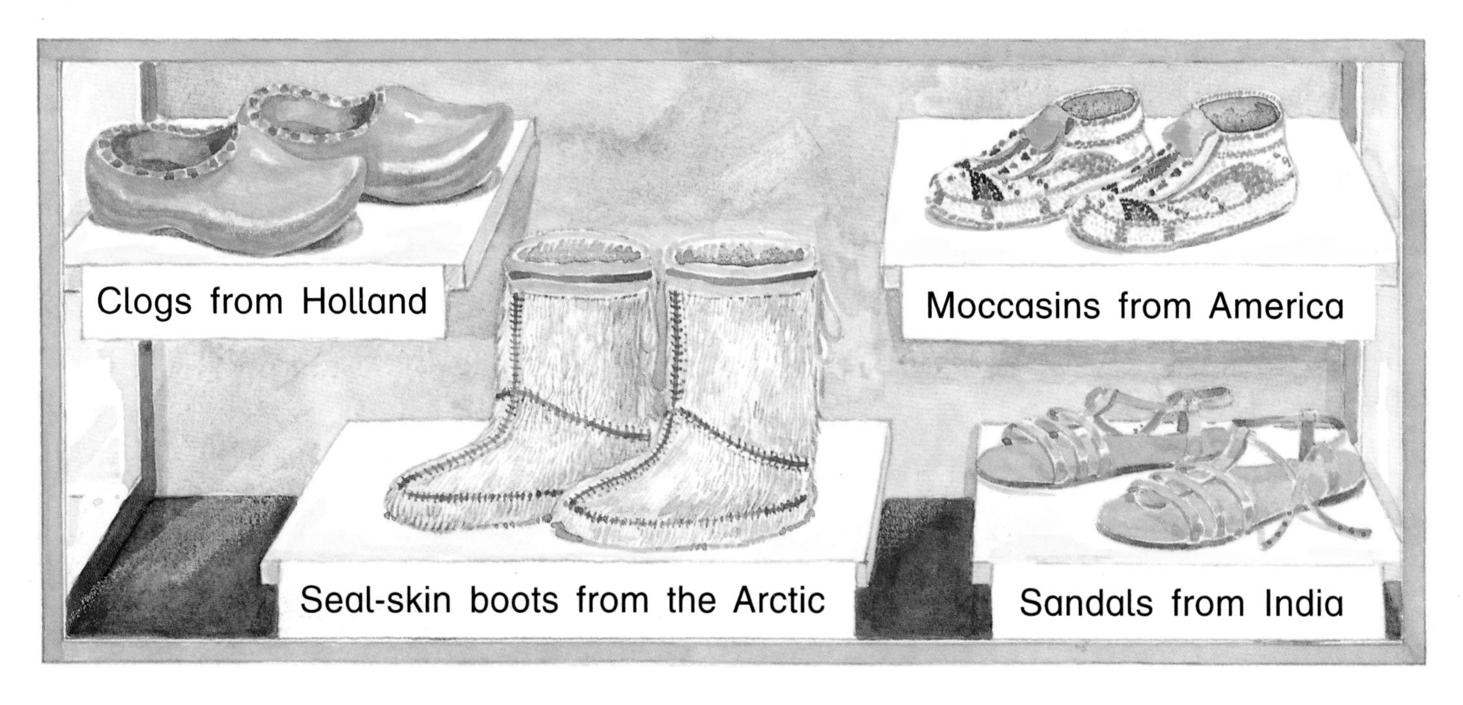

These shoes are from
different countries.
People wore these shoes long ago.

People had to make their own shoes.
They got the materials from
plants or animals.

Caring for leather shoes

First, undo the fasteners.

Next, brush off the dirt.

Then polish the shoes.

Finally, tidy them away.

Index

Oxford University Press,
Great Clarendon Street,
Oxford OX2 6DP

First published by Oxford University Press 1997

ISBN 0 19 916933 0

Available in packs
Clothes Pack (one of each title)
ISBN 0 19 916934 9
Clothes Class Pack (six of each title)
ISBN 0 19 916935 7

Acknowledgements

Illustrated by: Alex Brychta (p2); Celia Hart (pp7, 9); Jane Bottomley (pp12-13); Chris Smedley.

The Publisher would like to thank the following for permission to reproduce photographs: Allsport/Chris Raphael (p9); John Walmsley (p8 left).
All other photographs were taken by Martin Sookias.

Cover illustration: Chris Smedley.

Printed and bound in Hong Kong